The
Unsheltered
HEART

Father Ron Raab invites his readers to an Advent experience that will change them. His outstanding writing—lodged in his care for the women and men who make the street their home—is humble, provocative, and poignant. Prepare ye!

Jack Jezreel
Executive Director
JustFaith Ministries

"Put not your trust in princes," the prophets say. Father Raab urges love of the poor and the afflicted through conversion of our hearts—prompted by his profoundly challenging and distinctive Advent meditations.

Nicholas Ayo, C.S.C.
Author of *Gloria Patri*

In the opening lines of the first chapter, Raab dares his reader to pray, "O God, unshelter my heart." Most of us want God to shelter us, protect us, guard us, defend us. Raab suggests that what we really need is to become unsheltered, cracked open, deeply vulnerable—waking up to our solidarity with the suffering poor in whom God dwells.

Marilyn Lacey, R.S.M.
Author of *This Flowing Toward Me*

In a season when most of us are lulled into torpor by too much—food, drink, partying, shopping—Ron Raab's *The Unsheltered Heart* is a gentle but firm wake-up call to find our true selves in God by exposing our hearts to God's Word. The simple practical format will make it not another obligation, but a welcome respite for those wishing to deepen their Advent experience.

Bernadette Gasslein
Editor of *Celebrate! The Pastoral Magazine with the Liturgical Heart*

Cycle A

The Unsheltered HEART

an at-home advent retreat

Ronald Patrick Raab, c.s.c.

ave maria press AmP notre dame, indiana

© 2010 by Priests of Holy Cross, Indiana Province

All rights reserved. No part of this book may be used or reproduced in any manner whatsoever, except in the case of reprints in the context of reviews, without written permission from Ave Maria Press®, Inc., P.O. Box 428, Notre Dame, IN 46556.

Founded in 1865, Ave Maria Press is a ministry of the Indiana Province of Holy Cross.

www.avemariapress.com

ISBN-10 1-59471-254-9   ISBN-13 978-1-59471-254-8

Cover image © Malaika Favorite.

Cover and text design by Brian C. Conley.

Printed and bound in the United States of America.

In gratitude for all on the margins of society,
who teach me to believe in God's love.

Contents

Preface

Every year as Advent begins, I realize in the course of my ministry that the voices of the ancient prophets are still roaring for love and reform. I hear tales of longing, not only from the sacred scriptures, but also from the mouths of people living the effects of poverty and loss right in my own neighborhood. The loudest voices I hear cry for a chance to be heard, acknowledged, and understood. These voices—of people living on the streets, suffering mental illness, or struggling with various addictions—change my heart.

I carry these voices with me as I have carried the voices of the biblical prophets who roared for change. Often my heart grows cold from having neglected one or both of these groups—the boisterous ones of old or the quiet ones in our downtown Portland parish. My heart grows weary and dark as I hear people ask questions that I cannot answer or present problems that I cannot solve. I can't bring adequate health care to the destitute, solve housing needs for all the addicts, or keep people from selling their bodies on our street corner. I call these street voices "prophetic" because they shout to me, and to everyone in our culture, that many things need changing. Like those prophets of old, these contemporary prophets beg us to unshelter our hearts, to open and expose them to all in need so that we might hear their cry and heed their warnings. These unnamed prophets demand our attention as Advent dawns once again.

The biblical prophets remind us that the old will pass away and that new life is possible for everyone. These voices of Advent remind us that we do not wait for the Messiah, for God is already here among us. Rather, we wait for our hearts to wake up to love, which is, of course, the very presence of God among us. We wait for our hearts to be released from the shelter of fear, uncertainty, selfishness, and greed. We wait for love in the midst of our prejudice, our outbursts of anger, and the violence we do to others and to ourselves. This is the real Advent: discovering the rich voices of the prophets who roar in our hearts—hearts which perhaps have grown weary, silent, or even numb to genuine hope.

I shelter my heart from vulnerability to others when I work among people who do not have physical shelter. I protect my heart the most when I am among people who do not have the protection of homes, health care, or companionship. I fear loss in my own life as every person does. These experiences shape my life, my heart, and my prayer in these Advent days when we are called to open the gifts of our hearts to the people around us—no matter who they are or where they may sleep at night.

I do not glamorize poverty here. I do not live my faith vicariously among people in poverty. I write of my experiences because I discover the fear that lies deep within my heart as I minister among the marginalized of our society. This is the fear that shuts down love in my heart. It casts shadows on how I perceive people and releases a seething rage born of the realization that so many people do not have what they need in this life. This is my present experience of Advent: waiting among people who long to be heard, befriended, and loved.

This four-week retreat based on the Sunday gospel readings of Advent opens our hearts to deep longing for God and rich meaning for our own lives. The placement of these texts within the Eucharistic liturgy shapes our experiences of waking up to the reality of God's love for all people so as to discover our place in the world. I wrote this retreat so that you may uncover for yourself the fear that shields your heart and so that you will come to rest in God alone. This guide for daily reflection simply calls you to pay attention to your own experience, relationships, and priorities and ponder them in light of the Sunday gospels.

Introduction

Christmas preparations often exhaust people. Taking time for personal prayer, deep reflection, and restful quiet often comes at a great cost. However, not paying attention to the profound message that Advent instills in us costs us our awareness of one another's needs and our reassurance that God is at the center of all we wait for in life. This, too, is a great price to pay. The profound Sunday gospel readings of Advent can sift through our heart-stopping worry if we are willing to take a few minutes each day for prayer and reflection.

In addition to making time, another obstacle to prayer and the message of Advent comes in lingering loneliness. December rouses profound loneliness in many people. This loneliness crosses all economic boundaries. Our cultural expectations of always having happy families, abundant financial resources, healthy leisure, fulfilling employment, affirming friendships, and perfect love are not realistic for most of us. Christmas is especially difficult for anyone experiencing undiagnosed or untreated mental illness, recent or lingering unemployment, the death of a loved one, or any number of other new or ongoing life-upsetting hardships. At this time of year especially, so many people do not feel they are accepted among family. Many friendships become threadbare, and many people become emotionally crippled by loss and profound grief.

This holiday loneliness can even break us apart from the love of the Incarnation—from embracing the realization that God so loved the world that he sent us his only son. This retreat speaks to us of our real identity in Christ. I wrote it based on my experiences ministering among society's marginalized because God sought out the weak and vulnerable to offer tidings of joy. This is not an ultra-pious notion, but is the reality of Emmanuel, God with us.

This daily retreat is meant for all people of faith. I hope you will take the time to translate the gift of Advent through your own life experiences, in your family relationships, and even in your workplace. We all face the tragedy of loss, the unforgiving neighbor, the hurtful parent, the jealous co-worker, the angry spouse, and the unexpected illness. We all face the temptation to live with a shallow and well-guarded heart that protects us from life's hurts and frustrations. Advent prayer nudges us out of our self-concern and releases fear from our thoughts, attitudes, and faith.

The Advent prophets calling out in the Sunday gospel readings challenge us all to wake up to the love that is around us. Our daily reflection opens the gates of new life, hope, and love. We seek the unity of all people and the healing of our fragmented hearts in the coming of Christ Jesus, our Lord.

The Structure of This Retreat

Each week of this at-home retreat follows the same simple format. You are asked to read the Sunday gospel text not just on Sunday, but every day in order to stay focused and experience a deepening appreciation of its message to you. You will be prompted each day to respond in writing to the text, your reflection upon your life, and your encounter with God. Each day's retreat time ends with a prayer of your own creation, whether written or simply formed in the silence of your heart. This retreat unfolds in the following five steps.

Step 1. Welcome the Stranger Called Silence

December seldom invites time for personal silence. For most people, reflection time evaporates into preparing for family gatherings, making lists, shopping, attending required business parties, visiting with friends, and connecting with loved ones far away. Silence in this season often seems an unwelcome stranger.

I invite you to make sufficient time for silent prayer and reflection during these holy days of Advent. You will hear the gospel readings during Sunday Eucharist; but decision-making and planning are essential if you hope to set aside time to allow the readings to sink into your life patterns. The only way to hear the gospels and welcome the meaning of Advent and Christmas is to prepare a space in your life for silence. Prayer is a personal responsibility. My reflections here do not substitute for your prayer and silence. To begin taking responsibility for your prayer, prepare a comfortable space in your home where you can go to rest and reflect every day. Allow this setting to become your retreat place where you can offer God your private thoughts and authentic personal story, no matter how messy your story may be. The messages of Advent will come alive in the quiet minutes you spend in this place.

Step 2. Discover Your Story Within the Word

This retreat begins with the gospel readings from the Sunday celebration of the Eucharist. The simple lines of scripture embody the message of Christ for each person living today. Read, reflect, and ponder the passage every day during the week. Inspiration, grace, and love will flow through you when you take time to sit with God and the sacred text. Allow the events of your life to commune with God. Bring your lived story—the past and present—to the holy Word written centuries ago. You will find the echoes of God's voice rising up within your concerns, frustrations, and loneliness as well as in your joy. Open yourself to change within God's consolation and forgiveness. Unshelter your heart and let it rest in the presence of these gospel passages.

Step 3. Connect to the Waiting World: A Weekly Theme

Each week I offer a brief thematic essay in which I share connections between the message of the gospel story and my life experience. This reflection draws out the retreat theme for the week. It may not speak to your life, work, or place in the world; I simply present these words to spark your imagination. Think about your own life and find the links to the deeper story of Jesus and our faith tradition. If my reflections do not speak to you, then continue on, drawing more fully from your own experiences. This journal retreat is meant for you to relate to the gospel stories through reflection on your past and be open to God's grace for the future.

Step 4. Respond to the Cry of the Prophets

I continue to draw connections between the gospel reading and everyday life for each day of the week. Each day brings a deeper awareness of how the message of the gospel text is to be prayed, contemplated, and lived out. These reflections and invitations are meant to get you thinking about your own life and the people who surround you on a daily basis. If the daily reflection does not resonate with your personal story then do not pray with it, but explore your own experience to find solid ground from which to pray. Allow the rhythm of the daily reading of the scriptures to carve a path toward the coming of Christ in your own life.

For each day, I provide both questions for reflection and open-ended journaling statements to evoke more than a phrase or two from your life. I present these fill-in-the-blank sentences to prompt you to write about your thoughts, feelings, and reactions to the scriptures and your own life. These open-ended statements are the beginning of your real retreat. This journaling is where you may write honestly about your life and longing for the gift of God's presence. Writing will help you engage your actions, beliefs, patterns of behavior, and reflect on the ways in which you shelter your heart from being vulnerable to daily life. Write. Do not edit your words or worry about language or punctuation. If you enter into this process sincerely and prayerfully, this method of prayer will reveal your thoughts, concerns, worries, and fears.

Writing an action statement each day will come naturally from your own thoughts and prayers. Allow yourself to be deeply challenged about how you will live what you profess. Your prayer and God's grace will lead you to discover how you will act upon the insights you discover.

Step 5. Prayer: Writing Your Way to New Birth

The section called "Prayer" is offered each day to challenge your thinking about your relationship with God. I offer a prayer at the end of each week, which you may use to begin your own discernment and gather ideas for how to express what is going on in your relationship with God. But keep in mind that the genuine prayer of the retreat will flow from your written responses to the prompts mentioned in the fourth step.

Collect your insights and prayers in this booklet, your own journal, or even on scrap paper; and take time each day to compose your own prayer. Your written prayers do not need to be formal or follow any particular pattern. They may be just a few words, a sentence or two, or many words. Just write the words God gives you to open your heart. You may even find that your prayer comes without words. Write (if it helps), reflect, and pray in the way that becomes comfortable for you during your daily meditations.

Stay Awake!

SUNDAY

Step 1. Welcome the Stranger Called Silence
Settle into your retreat space and sit in silence for a minute or two.

Step 2. Discover Your Story Within the Word
As you make the sign of the cross, pray:

O God, unshelter my heart that I may hear and know your holy Word.

Read the gospel passage in silence or aloud.

Matthew 24:37–44
For as it was in the days of Noah, so it will be at the coming of the Son of Man.
In (those) days before the flood, they were eating and drinking, marrying and giving in marriage, up to the day that Noah entered the ark.
They did not know until the flood came and carried them all away. So will it be at the coming of the Son of Man.

7

**Two men will be out in the field; one will be taken,
and one will be left.
Two women will be grinding at the mill; one will
be taken, and one will be left.
Therefore, stay awake! For you do not know on
which day your Lord will come.
Be sure of this: if the master of the house had known
the hour of night when the thief was coming, he
would have stayed awake and not let his house be
broken into.
So too, you also must be prepared, for at an hour
you do not expect, the Son of Man will come.**

Spend another minute or two in silent reflection.

Step 3. Connect to the Waiting World: Stay Awake!

I wake up every day to people living in relationships that
are threatened or broken. I overhear the young mother begging
for someone to help her because her boyfriend is back in prison
and the streets are too violent for her infant son's survival. I listen to a middle-aged veteran tell me that he has not entered his
family's home in nearly thirty years. A survivor of heroin slowly
recaps his life to me as one by one all his friends and his family
have disowned him.

Waking up to people's stories is never easy for me. I learn,
however, that mustering the courage to receive a person's life is
always another moment of grace. I need to listen to the stranger
who finds herself severed from healthy relationships. These moments capture the real longing of people. These places of emptiness and despair carve out the place in which we all long for God
to be born. I dare not take anyone for granted because the next
relationship reveals the next lesson. These encounters teach me
that people cannot be judged, nor should their stories be stored in
some box and put on a shelf for later.

The authentic message for me in life and ministry is relationship. True and honest relationship is the core of Christianity. The reason for Christ's coming is simply to be in loving relationship with people. People enduring poverty become the Advent reminder for all of us that God aches to find us ready for faith and alert to others' needs. Among people living in poverty, the thief already has come. The robber is poverty itself, which strips away human dignity in the daylight. Poverty ravages the soul at night and leaves people vulnerable in early morning. Advent teaches me to build up the lives of people lost among the thieves of poverty, isolation, and neglect. In these moments, God is made visible, born among humanity.

I feel akin to the master of the house in Matthew's narrative. Regret and hand wringing are present—if unwritten—in the details of this story. If only he had stayed awake, the invasion into his house would not have happened. He lives in lament for his sleepiness—at not being attentive and present. Perhaps if he had stayed awake, he would have saved his belongings and treasures, and even the lives of other people.

I regret much about my limited ability to be present to people. If I only had paid more attention to that elderly man who just wanted to vent about his life, maybe he would not be so verbally outrageous. If I only had more resources, more money, or goods, then perhaps things could be different for the former prisoner who waits outside the chapel for clean clothing. If I only had more patience or kindness or more faith in God's investment in his believers, then maybe people living outside could find a home. These are the regrets I sort through in the early morning, much like the master of the house sorted through the wreckage after the thieves had carried off his valuables.

People's stories open up the real meaning of Advent. We wait for relationships to become right, balanced, and reconciled. We wait for equitable measures of goods, food, housing, clean water, and even love. We wait, knowing that only God can restore human relationships that are severed by violence or threatened by addictions, divorce, mental illness, aging, or disease. Advent is the time we begin to understand the story of Jesus from the perspective of the poverty of people's experiences, the poverty of the human condition. We wait for hope as we voice our despair so that God will hear the cries of his people. We wait for love as we serve people most in need of the basics of life. Perhaps this is the year that justice shall find its home on earth and peace will flourish among all relationships.

I wake up every day living in the tension of God's presence already on earth and yet still waiting for the fullness of Christ's return. God invites me to listen to the stranger and to trust that love is still being born in our time and place. I believe in the wake-up call of these four weeks of Advent when I stop regretting the lack of what I have to offer people no matter their background or how much money they possess. I still believe that God finds a home on earth when I stop judging others and honor the raw and cumbersome stories of everyday people. I trust that when I fully wipe the sleep from my eyes, I will see the miracles of God reconciling the lost and forgotten. I wait for the Advent day when I will be fully awake.

Step 4. Respond to the Cry of the Prophets

At first reading, this gospel cleaves our hearts like a strong ax. Jesus tells his disciples that people in the days of Noah were feeling secure. While they were enjoying the things of the earth, the flood came and changed their priorities. Everything that people had clung to for security was destroyed.

This gospel grabs our awareness in Advent because God longs for our total and undivided attention. God longs to be in relationship with our hearts no matter how lonely, shattered, or selfish they may be.

I invite you to take stock of your earthly possessions. How is the meaning of your life attached to what you own? Does what you own, in fact, own your complete attention? Begin this Advent week by sorting through your heart to identify what makes you feel secure and how willing you are to find a new security in God. Sit in silence with the thoughts of how you cling to things of the earth and how you resist the love of God. See how your prayer, thoughts, and attitudes bear real change.

1. I read the gospel today and my first reaction is

2. Jesus, I am afraid to ponder the meaning of my possessions because

3. Action: Today, I will sort out my attitudes about

Step 5. Prayer: Writing Your Way to New Birth

Take a minute or two to look back at what you have written. Then compose a short prayer offering whatever is in your heart to God. Write it in the space below or in the quiet of your heart and mind.

MONDAY

Step 1. Welcome the Stranger Called Silence
Settle into your retreat space and sit in silence for a minute or two.

Step 2. Discover Your Story Within the Word
As you make the sign of the cross, pray:

O God, unshelter my heart that I may hear and know your holy Word.

Read the Sunday gospel passage (pp. 7–8) in silence or aloud. Then spend another minute or two in silent reflection on the reading.

To what spiritual realities are you waking up today?

Step 3. Connect to the Waiting World: Stay Awake!
You may wish to revisit the thematic essay on pages 8–10 if it will help you focus your retreat time.

Take a couple of minutes to think about how well you did with your action from yesterday. Journal about it if that is useful.

Step 4. *Respond to the Cry of the Prophets*

The gospel story invites us into sharing belief with people who have suffered great loss. The people in Noah's day experienced the flood, and every earthly thing changed. Loss in life is never easy nor anticipated. The message of Advent opens us to God's new presence when we bear the most human of all suffering—loss and emptiness. God tries to open hearts that are shut down by human tragedy.

I invite you to offer some quiet moments to allow the words of the gospel to capture your heart. Allow its message to rise up in you and open your thoughts toward what losses you have known. Ponder how you have handled losing a job, a home, a friend, your reputation, your financial savings, or your good health. Allow your heart to rest in the security of God's love for you.

1. God, I bring to your life today my loss and I

2. As I reflect back on my life, I realize that my reactions to my losses have

3. Action: Today, I will forgive and let go of

Step 5. Prayer: Writing Your Way to New Birth

Take a minute or two to look back at what you have written. Then compose a short prayer offering whatever is in your heart to God. Write it in the space below or in the quiet of your heart and mind.

TUESDAY

Step 1. Welcome the Stranger Called Silence

Settle into your retreat space and sit in silence for a minute or two.

Step 2. Discover Your Story Within the Word

As you make the sign of the cross, pray:

O God, unshelter my heart that I may hear and know your holy Word.

Read the Sunday gospel passage in silence or aloud. Then spend another minute or two in silent reflection on the reading. To what spiritual realities are you waking up today?

Step 3. Connect to the Waiting World: Stay Awake!

Reflect on your action from yesterday.

How well have you met that goal?

Step 4. Respond to the Cry of the Prophets

The gospel reading explains that a change in relationships occurred in the time of the flood. One man was left in the field and another was taken. One woman was left grinding at the mill and the other was taken.

Advent tries to name human loss and suffering so that all can come to terms with a new need and longing for God. At the deepest levels of our hearts, only God can enter and change what is lost, abandoned, and neglected.

I invite you to reflect now on the people you love and whom you call your friends and family. Sit and ponder each name in prayerful silence. Bring their faces to your thoughts. Treasure the gifts of the people around you today. Be aware of the hardships, trials, and changes they have lived through this year.

1. When I cling too strongly to relationships, I usually

2. I long to trust God more profoundly as I face changes in

3. Action: Today, I will contact my long-lost friend

Step 5. Prayer: Writing Your Way to New Birth

Take a minute or two to look back at what you have written. Then compose a short prayer offering whatever is in your heart to God. Write it in the space below or in the quiet of your heart and mind.

■ WEDNESDAY

Step 1. Welcome the Stranger Called Silence

Settle into your retreat space and sit in silence for a minute or two.

Step 2. Discover Your Story Within the Word

As you make the sign of the cross, pray:

O God, unshelter my heart that I may hear and know your holy Word.

Read the Sunday gospel passage in silence or aloud. Then spend another minute or two in silent reflection on the reading. To what spiritual realities are you waking up today?

Step 3. Connect to the Waiting World: Stay Awake!

Reflect on your action from yesterday

How well have you met that goal?

Step 4. *Respond to the Cry of the Prophets*

In the gospel narrative, the master of the house experienced unexpected suffering. The thief broke into his home in the night. The master, of course, was asleep, unaware of what was happening to his home.

Advent is not just a cozy reminder that Christmas is coming soon. Advent penetrates our notions that our reliance on God must be steadfast, secure, and long-lived. Here we reflect again on how our hearts bear the pain that often shuts us down from God's love within us.

Today's reading of the gospel encourages your insights into how you have managed sudden and unexpected suffering. I invite you to consider the unanticipated failures, the breaks in friendship, or times of dishonesty among family members, which you faced during this past year. Open your heart to how you managed your pain beyond anger, fret, and worry. Pray through these moments to allow your heart to be open to an even deeper trust in God.

1. Today, I am able to accept

2. God, help me sort out the suffering that still shuts down my heart so that

3. Action: Today, I will review my life and

Step 5. Prayer: Writing Your Way to New Birth

Take a minute or two to look back at what you have written. Then compose a short prayer offering whatever is in your heart to God. Write it in the space below or in the quiet of your heart and mind.

THURSDAY

Step 1. Welcome the Stranger Called Silence

Settle into your retreat space and sit in silence for a minute or two.

Step 2. Discover Your Story Within the Word

As you make the sign of the cross, pray:

O God, unshelter my heart that I may hear and know your holy Word.

Read the Sunday gospel passage in silence or aloud. Then spend another minute or two in silent reflection on the reading. To what spiritual realities are you waking up today?

Step 3. Connect to the Waiting World: Stay Awake!
Reflect on your action from yesterday.
How well have you met that goal?

Step 4. Respond to the Cry of the Prophets

Jesus demands that we prepare ourselves for the coming of the Son of Man. We live in this expectation of Christ's return. This preparation for Christ is at the heart of the Advent message. This preparation comes in opening our fragile hearts to God's passion and love.

Advent allows us to become more focused and intentional about how we live our lives on earth. We live each day in anticipation of God's love and grace, yet we know that we already dwell in the all-embracing presence of God.

Consider how you are preparing yourself emotionally and prayerfully, not only for Christmas, but also for Christ's return. How does your prayer reflect your appreciation of your life? How do you learn through your life circumstances to trust God for all you need in life? Examine the attitudes, the scars, and the emotional pain you carry with you. Christ will come when least expected. Prayerfully consider that all you need in life is what you have today.

1. Jesus, help me to prepare for a deeper relationship with you by

2. God, allow me a new attitude toward

3.   Action: Today, I will sort out my negative attitudes about myself and

Step 5. Prayer: Writing Your Way to New Birth

Take a minute or two to look back at what you have written. Then compose a short prayer offering whatever is in your heart to God. Write it in the space below or in the quiet of your heart and mind.

■ FRIDAY

Step 1. Welcome the Stranger Called Silence

Settle into your retreat space and sit in silence for a minute or two.

Step 2. Discover Your Story Within the Word

As you make the sign of the cross, pray:

O God, unshelter my heart that I may hear and know your holy Word.

Read the Sunday gospel passage in silence or aloud. Then spend another minute or two in silent reflection on the reading. To what spiritual realities are you waking up today?

Step 3. *Connect to the Waiting World: Stay Awake!*
Reflect on your action from yesterday.

How well have you met that goal?

Step 4. *Respond to the Cry of the Prophets*

The message of Christ rouses us from sleep—from not pay ing attention to the life God is offering us. Advent invites us to open our eyes and become aware with our souls to the stirrings of God within every aspect of life.

Advent calls us into the world with wide eyes. These weeks of preparation are meant to get us in touch with the core needs of the world. Advent creates room for God to create a new earth, beginning with us.

I invite you to consider your own sleepy ways. Take into account all the areas of your life in which you feel you are not fully awake. Ponder how you may have become numb to the hardships and tragedies of the world such as hunger, violence, and war. Take into your prayer the people you avoid and the situations in which you are not paying attention to others. Consider how you are asleep to your own needs as well. Allow your heart to rest in a new watchfulness, a new reliance on God's mercy for you.

1. Jesus, receive my skepticism, my sleepiness, so that

2. Jesus, only you can break through my bashful heart and

3. Action: Today I will wake up to the needs of those I love and

Step 5. Prayer: Writing Your Way to New Birth

Take a minute or two to look back at what you have written. Then compose a short prayer offering whatever is in your heart to God. Write it in the space below or in the quiet of your heart and mind.

SATURDAY

Step 1. Welcome the Stranger Called Silence

Settle into your retreat space and sit in silence for a minute or two.

Step 2. Discover Your Story Within the Word

As you make the sign of the cross, pray:

O God, unshelter my heart that I may hear and know your holy Word.

Read the Sunday gospel passage in silence or aloud. Then spend another minute or two in silent reflection on the reading. To what spiritual realities are you waking up today?

Step 3. Connect to the Waiting World: Stay Awake!
Reflect on your action from yesterday.

How well have you met that goal?

Step 4. Respond to the Cry of the Prophets

Jesus' strong message to stay awake continues to ring in our hearts. His decisive words declaring that his presence will change everything echo across the generations. His forceful words to stay awake mean we should cultivate a new desire for God alone. Our human vulnerability is awakened to God's fidelity and strength for us all.

Advent grace claims our hearts. We are meant to live a new vulnerability in God's love and concern for us. This is what we wait for in the full celebration of Christmas—to live with an unprotected heart so that we may discover that God is already born deep within our hearts, concerns, and longings.

Consider today what it means for you to stay awake for God. Ponder this Advent message of opening your eyes, emotions, thoughts, hopes, and desires to the passion of God. God longs for the best for you. God desires to be in a loving relationship with you. God wishes you to wake up and see that your life is more than the pain, suffering, and hardship you endure or the complacency that keeps you comfortable. Wake up! Stay awake until the Lord's coming.

1. Today, I fear waking up to the reality of life because

2. God, open your life to me even in my sleepiness and lack of attention so that

3. Action: Today I will admit I need God and so

Step 5. Prayer: Writing Your Way to New Birth

Take a minute or two to look back at what you have written. Then compose a short prayer offering whatever is in your heart to God. Write it in the space below or in the quiet of your heart and mind.

Prayer for the First Week of Advent

Jesus,
This faded blue chair carries my sheltered heart.
As dawn creeps up, the sounds of sirens screech
through my silence here.
My prayer casts its shadow among the homeless lining
up outside, under my window.

I protect my heart from the cigarette-born coughs I
hear outside.
The sounds of shouts, threats, and rage push against
my windowpane.
The noise of all humanity I caress around my soul.

My silent shouts scream out at you to change us all.
My deeper silence uncovers my fear to speak up, as the
ancient prophets did.
I now understand why they shouted out—because life
is so unfair.

I hold the heavy bible on my lap and feel the weight of
belief.
The Word is no longer a stranger as I hear the voices on
the busy streets.
Morning rises now on my generation and you call us all
to "stay awake!"
Amen.

Make Straight His Paths

SUNDAY

Step 1. Welcome the Stranger Called Silence
Settle into your retreat space and sit in silence for a minute or two.

Step 2. Discover Your Story Within the Word
As you make the sign of the cross, pray:

O God, unshelter my heart that I may hear and know your holy Word.

Read the gospel passage in silence or aloud.

Matthew 3:1–12
In those days John the Baptist appeared, preaching in the desert of Judea saying, "Repent, for the kingdom of heaven is at hand!"
It was of him that the prophet Isaiah had spoken when he said: "A voice of one crying out in the desert, 'Prepare the way of the Lord, make straight his paths.'"
John wore clothing made of camel's hair and had a leather belt around his waist. His food was locusts and wild honey.

At that time Jerusalem, all Judea, and the whole region around the Jordan were going out to him and were being baptized by him in the Jordan River as they acknowledged their sins.

When he saw many of the Pharisees and Sadducees coming to his baptism, he said to them, "You brood of vipers! Who warned you to flee from the coming wrath? Produce good fruit as evidence of your repentance. And do not presume to say to yourselves, 'We have Abraham as our father.' For I tell you, God can raise up children to Abraham from these stones.

Even now the ax lies at the root of the trees. Therefore every tree that does not bear good fruit will be cut down and thrown into the fire.

I am baptizing you with water, for repentance, but the one who is coming after me is mightier than I. I am not worthy to carry his sandals. He will baptize you with the Holy Spirit and fire.

His winnowing fan is in his hand. He will clear his threshing floor and gather his wheat into his barn, but the chaff he will burn with unquenchable fire."

Spend another minute or two in silent reflection on the reading.

Step 3. Connect to the Waiting World: Make Straight His Paths

I spend my day in the swirl of people's unanswerable questions. There are no satisfying words that will solve the heartache of the mother of three children who now scrapes by financially after her husband has left the family. There are no defined solutions or satisfactory explanations to solve the mystery of why a twelve-year-old girl faces the horror of cancer. There are no formulaic answers or automatic certainties that I can offer to a couple who have just lost their son to suicide. I listen carefully to the message of John the Baptist in Advent, and he slowly convinces me that I must rely on Christ once again.

I desire John's urgency for myself. He called people to change their hearts and lives, not out of fear, but conviction that Jesus would bring a deeper love for all humanity. He challenged people to set new priorities, not because they would be condemned, but because he did not want them to miss the love that God was offering them. His unwavering priority demonstrated by his simple clothing and his modest diet showed that his entire life pointed in the direction of Christ Jesus.

This action of pointing in the direction of Christ is not always easy. I still want to control God's responses and help solve people's mysteries myself. I still hesitate to let go of my own power because my convictions about Christ are still weak and unsteady. I bring this weariness to my contemplation of John, and he wakes me up again to the reality that I am not in charge of anyone's life. I must see for myself in these days of Advent that only grace changes my perspective on how I live and how I view other people.

In Advent, I realize that if I am going to live in the tension of others' unanswered questions then I cannot live my faith in isolation. John points me to the Body of Christ. He brings me back to community. In Advent, he teaches me that my conviction of faith will only mean something to others if it is lived among people. This is the place of tension and yet real faith for me. I must rely on the presence of Christ within the community to live out the questions of life that are often unanswerable. In other words, I must rely on something greater than myself.

The community then becomes the place of challenge to push the boundaries of justice as well as the place where compassion and love are already present. If I am going to bring the difficult questions of life to Christ, then that means I bring those questions to the community as well. Like John, we are to live unselfconsciously serving people in real need. We are to collect our common voices and speak out for the weak, the vulnerable, and the lost among us. We are to give ourselves relentlessly for the sake of God's kingdom.

The message of John continues to show us that Christmas is not just for the well educated, the well dressed, or the unquestioning believer. The real passion for Christ comes in believing that our communities are to remain vigilant and strong so that the weak will find a home. We are to let go of our preconceived ideas about many of our neighbors who suffer beyond our imagining. Each community must deal with the vulnerable who make their way to the church door and the sick who are isolated behind our gated communities. We are to tend to the secrets we all carry in our hearts, and the notion that we do not really belong to God. We are to welcome the immigrant and stranger, the suburban addict and the veteran suffering great depression. We are to learn from John the Baptist not to take more than we need in life and be satisfied with the gifts that come from God.

John's voice is not easily heard or understood in Advent. I am confident that the companies that print Christmas cards would not remain in business if John the Baptist were the only image of Christmas preparation. In the center of cultural expectations of what Christmas is supposed to be, John does not rank among the cozy, comfortable images of the season. However, John calls us back to the authentic reasons why Jesus was once born in our midst and continues his saving work even in our day.

My ministry among our culture's most fragile people teaches me to carry Christ in my heart as the priority in my life. When I open myself to the raw needs of others in my faith community, I hear and understand the message of John calling me to wake from my slumber of self-reliance and apathy. John's challenge is alive today calling us to live our priority of being Christ amid the unanswerable questions of our lives.

Step 4. Respond to the Cry of the Prophets

John the Baptist cries out to us all to repent of our past failures. His voice harkens above even our deepest sins to create a new path toward the beauty and goodness of God. Here John invites us into honest and loving forgiveness with God and our neighbor.

The gospel reading of the second week of Advent stresses the importance of John's role in pointing us all toward Christ. John, the great prophet, stirs in our hearts the reality of God's presence in Christ Jesus.

I invite you into deep reflection on any guilt or shame you hold in your heart. These aspects of the human heart shield us from the real love we desire. We even protect ourselves from Christ's love when shame, guilt, or anger takes hold of us. John invites us to acknowledge the sin or offense that may be closing down our relationships with God and even with ourselves. Allow God to heal you during these rich days of Advent grace. Allowing God to penetrate the hardness of our hearts—the protection we build around ourselves—is part of our waiting for new life in this Advent season.

1. John the Baptist challenges me to face

2. My prayer today seems

3. Action: Today I will admit my negative thoughts and attitudes about

Step 5. Prayer: Writing Your Way to New Birth
Take a minute or two to look back at what you have written. Then compose a short prayer offering whatever is in your heart to God. Write it in the space below or in the quiet of your heart and mind.

MONDAY

Step 1. Welcome the Stranger Called Silence
Settle into your retreat space and sit in silence for a minute or two.

Step 2. Discover Your Story Within the Word
As you make the sign of the cross, pray:

O God, unshelter my heart that I may hear and know your holy Word.

Read the Sunday gospel passage (pp. 27–28) in silence or aloud. Then spend another minute or two in silent reflection on the reading.

In what ways are you helping to make straight the way for God's justice?

Step 3. Connect to the Waiting World: Make Straight His Paths

You may wish to revisit the thematic essay on pages 28–30 if it will help you focus your retreat time.

Take a couple of minutes to think about how well you did with your action from yesterday. Journal about it if that is useful.

Step 4. Respond to the Cry of the Prophets

In today's reading of the scripture, John the Baptist commands us to change our ways. He tells us at the top of his voice to straighten our paths, open our hearts, and live for the coming of the kingdom of heaven.

John's message to change our ways may come as simply recognizing the needs of people around us. We listen to people when they need a sounding board, respond to them when life overwhelms them, and care for them when times are difficult. This path of knowing that others are in need around us creates a straight path to God.

I invite you to consider prayerfully the people that knock on your door and heart asking you for friendship and a helping hand. I am not asking you to solve every problem or to discover a solution for every need. Here, ponder in prayer how you open yourself to others on the journey to God. Pray through the changes you might make in your life to ready your heart for the kingdom of heaven, knowing that loved ones and strangers are also walking with you.

1. Jesus, today as change knocks on my door, I will consider

2. God, comfort those I love so

3. Action: Today, I will provide for a stranger so

Step 5. Prayer: Writing Your Way to New Birth

Take a minute or two to look back at what you have written. Then compose a short prayer offering whatever is in your heart to God. Write it in the space below or in the quiet of your heart and mind.

TUESDAY

Step 1. Welcome the Stranger Called Silence

Settle into your retreat space and sit in silence for a minute or two.

Step 2. Discover Your Story Within the Word

As you make the sign of the cross, pray:

O God, unshelter my heart that I may hear and know your holy Word.

Read the Sunday gospel passage in silence or aloud. Then spend another minute or two in silent reflection on the reading.

In what ways are you helping to make straight the way for God's justice?

Step 3. Connect to the Waiting World: Make Straight His Paths

Reflect on your action from yesterday.

How well have you met that goal?

Step 4. Respond to the Cry of the Prophets

The voice of John rattles even the desert silence. His strong presence comes to us across generations to challenge our faith, waken our priorities, and set us on a straight course to God. His voice is often more than our ears or hearts are ready to hear.

Advent sets us on track to hear the real and passionate voice of God. However, we all have many competing voices in our lives trying to get our attention. Our children's voices cry out to us in need every day. People at our workplace need our input at this very second. Our daily schedules, car pools, extended families, and work responsibilities can make us deaf to the real voices of change within us.

I encourage you to sort out the voices that you most need to listen to at this time in your life. Prepare your day in silent prayer so that you can discern these voices, these challenges to listen and change your priorities. John's voice rings in our daily priority in this Advent season.

1. John, point me into a new direction of

2. God, the pain of others that wears me down is

3. Action: Today, I will go out of my way to listen to

Step 5. Prayer: Writing Your Way to New Birth

Take a minute or two to look back at what you have written. Then compose a short prayer offering whatever is in your heart to God. Write it in the space below or in the quiet of your heart and mind.

WEDNESDAY

Step 1. Welcome the Stranger Called Silence
Settle into your retreat space and sit in silence for a minute or two.

Step 2. Discover Your Story Within the Word
As you make the sign of the cross, pray:

O God, unshelter my heart that I may hear and know your holy Word.

Read the Sunday gospel passage in silence or aloud. Then spend another minute or two in silent reflection on the reading.

In what ways are you helping to make straight the way for God's justice?

Step 3. Connect to the Waiting World: Make Straight His Paths
Reflect on your action from yesterday.

How well have you met that goal?

Step 4. Respond to the Cry of the Prophets
John's action and voice in the gospel ring a note of authentic simplicity and honesty. He comes from the desert wearing modest clothing, and scarcely eating. His message comes in an uncomplicated form that may be threatening to us even today. He comes with straightforwardness of action, words, and lifestyle.

We all struggle at this time of year to make the Advent season meaningful to those we love and to our communities of faith. I invite you to consider how the simplicity and directness of John's message may be a way of living out the call of love, patience, and integrity even today.

Consider prayerfully how you are living a life of simplicity. Listen to your own words and how they speak of this honesty. Review your life and ask yourself if you take more than you need in life and, if so, in what areas. Consider the ways your actions speak to others of a simple reliance on God. Pray through the purchasing choices you make this season and the choices you make in setting priorities for your family.

1. Jesus, help me hear the authentic voice of

2. God, the real value of my giving gifts is

3. Action: I will consider a simpler giving this year because

Step 5. Prayer: Writing Your Way to New Birth

Take a minute or two to look back at what you have written. Then compose a short prayer offering whatever is in your heart to God. Write it in the space below or in the quiet of your heart and mind.

THURSDAY ∎

Step 1. Welcome the Stranger Called Silence
Settle into your retreat space and sit in silence for a minute or two.

Step 2. Discover Your Story Within the Word
As you make the sign of the cross, pray:

O God, unshelter my heart that I may hear and know your holy Word.

Read the Sunday gospel passage in silence or aloud. Then spend another minute or two in silent reflection on the reading.

In what ways are you helping to make straight the way for God's justice?

Step 3. Connect to the Waiting World: Make Straight His Paths
Reflect on your action from yesterday.

How well have you met that goal?

Step 4. Respond to the Cry of the Prophets
John challenges us to produce good fruit in our efforts to change our ways. The strength of his conviction opens our hearts for the path of Christ's coming. The love we seek comes from God. The fruit of that love is revealed in how we love other people.

Advent grace also allows us to harvest the rich love we have known throughout the past year. This rich fruit of God's care, compassion, and love comes to us this season in those who love us and those who wait for our caring and concern.

I suggest today that you acknowledge the goodness of your life—not just the simple acts you accomplish, but also the deep abiding love that resounds in your heart as a child of God. The love we need already exists within our hearts. God is already among us. Tap into that love and passion today in your silence. Be grateful for all that is in your life and in the world. Allow John's words of being "good fruit" to open your heart to the wonder of God in your life and in the lives of those you love.

1. Jesus, I am grateful for the good fruit within me that

2. I long to be pruned of my misunderstandings that

3. Action: I will prune away my negative thoughts and be grateful today for

Step 5. Prayer: Writing Your Way to New Birth

Take a minute or two to look back at what you have written. Then compose a short prayer offering whatever is in your heart to God. Write it in the space below or in the quiet of your heart and mind.

FRIDAY

Step 1. Welcome the Stranger Called Silence

Settle into your retreat space and sit in silence for a minute or two.

Step 2. Discover Your Story Within the Word

As you make the sign of the cross, pray:

O God, unshelter my heart that I may hear and know your holy Word.

Read the Sunday gospel passage in silence or aloud. Then spend another minute or two in silent reflection on the reading.

In what ways are you helping to make straight the way for God's justice?

Step 3. *Connect to the Waiting World: Make Straight His Paths*
Reflect on your action from yesterday.

How well have you met that goal?

Step 4. *Respond to the Cry of the Prophets*

John's call to bear fruit also comes with many choices that we need to make every day. These choices may allow our hearts to be open, or we may find that our choices close the pathway to God. Life itself will bear the fruit of how we work through many of our life choices.

Advent continues to show us the way to God. We dig deep into the soil of our lives and plant firmly within our hearts a love that will last. However, we are human and our choices always need to be re-evaluated. Because we are weak, God makes us strong in Christ Jesus.

I invite you to reflect on some of the major choices you have made this year. How have you seen the grace and fruit of these choices? Which ones would you consider changing if life could offer such a choice? Which ones do you think were wrong choices? This time of year is a gift for you to reflect on the fact that no matter what choices you have made, God is there in the center of your life as it exits today. Regardless of your efforts, God's love and the fruit of grace will be revealed if you are open to this gift.

1. Jesus, I carry the failures around in my heart and I ask you

2. Jesus, unmask my heart and help me acknowledge
my choices of (or to)

3. Action: I now know I need to

Step 5. Prayer: Writing Your Way to New Birth

Take a minute or two to look back at what you have written. Then compose a short prayer offering whatever is in your heart to God. Write it in the space below or in the quiet of your heart and mind.

SATURDAY

Step 1. Welcome the Stranger Called Silence
Settle into your retreat space and sit in silence for a minute or two.

Step 2. Discover Your Story Within the Word
As you make the sign of the cross, pray:

O God, unshelter my heart that I may hear and know your holy Word.

Read the Sunday gospel passage in silence or aloud. Then spend another minute or two in silent reflection on the reading.

In what ways are you helping to make straight the way for God's justice?

Step 3. Connect to the Waiting World: Make Straight His Paths
Reflect on your action from yesterday.

How well have you met that goal?

Step 4. Respond to the Cry of the Prophets

John baptized Jesus while not feeling worthy to do even something so lowly as carry Christ's sandals. Yet it was John who announced that Jesus would baptize with the Holy Spirit and with fire. John hardly felt worthy of being the forerunner of Jesus, the one in whom salvation rests.

Advent grace floods our souls with water and fire. We can capture within us the love of God, a true blaze that will never be extinguished. This fire of passion and love unshackles our hearts and frees us to serve Christ in every thought, action, and circumstance of life.

Today, in your reflection on this week's gospel reading, I encourage you to find the fire in your life. Where is the passion in you for life, for good, for hope, and ultimately for God? How is John pointing to you to be a prophet of God, to set the world aflame with hope? How is Jesus still baptizing you with goodness, creativity, and a discovery of your own gifts in the world? In your prayer today, pray for a new fire of hope because the world is depending on you to be a praiseworthy believer in Christ Jesus.

1. Jesus, send a new fire into my life so that

2. John, help me point my life into the direction of God so that I

3. Action: I will affirm my own gifts and talents today as God's gifts to me by

Step 5. Prayer: Writing Your Way to New Birth

Take a minute or two to look back at what you have written Then compose a short prayer offering whatever is in your heart to God. Write it in the space below or in the quiet of your heart and mind.

Prayer for the Second Week of Advent

Jesus,
The cold air swirls around my rigid body this morning.
I feel my tightened chest and short breaths straddling
my silence.
I want to flee this chair because I know my
shortcomings.

I still live wanting desperately to control life's
outcomes.
People's unsolved questions pile up here around my
hesitant prayer.
My shallow quiet reveals my lack of trust that you hear
people's pleas.

I go further into my fear and find my stubbornness to
let you love me.
I hear the prophet's quest for reform and feel only my
heart's calluses.
My Advent ache rouses a new desire for you to listen
to my unanswered fear.

I hear the shouts of John and feel his quest for your fire.
You have baptized me in life's suffering and
uncertainty.
Warm my spirit with your assurance that good fruit
will be born in me.
Amen

Go and Tell What You Hear and See

SUNDAY

Step 1. Welcome the Stranger Called Silence
Settle into your retreat space and sit in silence for a minute or two.

Step 2. Discover Your Story Within the Word
As you make the sign of the cross, pray:

O God, unshelter my heart that I may hear and know your holy Word.

Read the gospel passage in silence or aloud.

Matthew 11:2–11
When John heard in prison of the works of the Messiah, he sent his disciples to him with this question, "Are you the one who is to come, or should we look for another?"
Jesus said to them in reply, "Go and tell John what you hear and see:
the blind regain their sight, the lame walk, lepers

are cleansed, the deaf hear, the dead are raised, and the poor have the good news proclaimed to them. And blessed is the one who takes no offense at me." As they were going off, Jesus began to speak to the crowds about John, "What did you go out to the desert to see? A reed swayed by the wind? Then what did you go out to see? Someone dressed in fine clothing? Those who wear fine clothing are in royal palaces. Then why did you go out? To see a prophet? Yes, I tell you, and more than a prophet. This is the one about whom it is written: 'Behold, I am sending my messenger ahead of you; he will prepare your way before you.' Amen, I say to you, among those born of women there has been none greater than John the Baptist; yet the least in the kingdom of heaven is greater than he.

Spend another minute or two in silent reflection on the reading.

Step 3. Connect to the Waiting World: Go and Tell What You Hear and See

I wait with people living in poverty who long for good news. I wait for the middle-aged man—beaten up during the night as he slept in a doorway—to find a shower today and health care and employment tomorrow. I wait for sobriety for a pregnant teenager. I long for affordable housing for the elderly woman who just lost her husband to a fast-growing cancer. I wait with many people who suffer poverty to find in our communities our call to serve other people.

These are also the stories that teach me not to despair. I discover on most days that I am the one who wants to flee from God and find other answers to life. I grow more impatient toward injustice, the way we treat the elderly, and our lack of care for people suffering mental illness. I shake my fists, lash out with violent words, and weep amid people's pain. If I have the patience to actually listen to people, to hear their soft-spoken stories, I usually find a profound love of God and their sincere trust in Christ.

Advent awakens our faith through people who have been marginalized. This week's gospel reading teaches us that the witnesses to Jesus are people whom society has already cast aside. Jesus tells us to listen to the person who we thought was deaf because now she will teach us how to really listen. Jesus says go to the person who you assumed could not walk and he will show you the more honest path to the Father. Learn to see the blind man whom you ignored before and he will open your eyes to faith and the reality of the Gospel itself. Jesus says that we should take a lesson from the leper who was isolated from everyone she loved: she will teach us how to care for people living on the margins of our culture.

One of the lessons I learn from this passage of Matthew is that there is rejoicing on the way to Christ's coming again. Christ did not promise to take away our suffering, but he did promise to remain with us forever. I grow weary of our culture's lack of response to people living in poverty. My heart is downcast as we continue to discriminate against certain people, make unhelpful judgments about others, and blame many innocent people for their painful predicaments. I also learn a profound gratitude from people who are actually experiencing these upheavals, illnesses, and uncertainties.

I hear sincere gratitude for a clean pair of underwear from a man who just hitchhiked into town looking for employment. I listen carefully to another story of thankfulness from a homeless single mother who needs formula for her newborn. One morning I wanted to give an elderly man another pair of socks, but he kindly refused them. I realized my offering was simply to make me feel better about my ability to give him more things. Then something happened to me. I realized that I had not been grateful for anything in days. I am often caught by the realization that I cannot minister to satisfy my own needs. Only then does gratitude become my heart's rejoicing. Advent hope runs deep within the human condition. The ache for a better life begins with a new gratitude for even our weakest moments. People without power in our culture bear witness to this new life, and I witness this miracle in ministry among our culture's marginalized. With nearly every encounter, individuals tell me that they need only one pair of socks or one shirt or just one small tube of toothpaste. Hope swells in me when my pretense, my sense of entitlement, my false authority, and my assumption that I know what is best for other people begin to fade away. Advent hope corrects my false claim that I am in charge of life and changes my errant belief that God is an intellectual pursuit. Advent hope runs underneath the anger, the rage, and the frustrations that surface in my attempts to fix other people's problems.

The ill, the marginalized, and the suffering all bear witness to the claim that Jesus is the one for whom everyone is searching. I keep an eye on Christ, even as I start to look for something else in life to fix my own needs and those of other people. If I don't keep my watch on Christ, I grow bitter, cynical, and unsure of my place in God's love. Without witness to Christ's presence and what he is doing, I have nothing left to give anyone. So I keep one eye on Christ even when I grow tired of searching for his presence. I hold on to this good news even though it remains quiet and elusive amid the loud noises of the aching world.

Step 4. Respond to the Cry of the Prophets

The third Sunday of Advent traditionally evokes rejoicing because we have journeyed half way to the promise of Christmas. We hear first the words of John making sure that it is the Christ we are following, and that we need not look for another source of salvation.

Advent invites us deep within the human condition to acknowledge the real meaning of why we wait for Christ. John's question opens our hearts to make sure we are focused on the one who will bring glad tidings to the poor and lonely.

In your reflection on the gospel reading today, I encourage you to ask, "Where am I looking for life?" Is it possible in thi*

Advent season that we are still looking in the wrong places—such as our addictions—to justify our worth? Do we still believe that money, prestige, and recognition will sustain us? Be honest with yourself today. Are you looking for life within your own heart? Or do you seek meaning through material goods or what you can purchase for others? Take time to sit with John's question and be grateful for your life.

1. I am always looking for a quick fix to change

2. I am never sure of myself in relationship to others, so I tend to

3. Action: Today, I will actively be grateful for

Step 5. Prayer: Writing Your Way to New Birth

Take a minute or two to look back at what you have written. Then compose a short prayer offering whatever is in your heart to God. Write it in the space below or in the quiet of your heart and mind.

∎ MONDAY

Step 1. Welcome the Stranger Called Silence
Settle into your retreat space and sit in silence for a minute or two.

Step2. Discover Your Story Within the Word
As you make the sign of the cross, pray:

O God, unshelter my heart that I may hear and know your holy Word.

Read the Sunday gospel passage (pp. 49–50) in silence or aloud. Then spend another minute or two in silent reflection on the reading.

What good news do you see and hear that you can tell others?

Step 3. Connect to the Waiting World: Go and Tell What You Hear and See
You may wish to revisit the thematic essay on pages 50–52 if it will help you focus your retreat time.

Take a couple of minutes to think about how well you did with your action from yesterday. Journal about it if that is useful.

Step 4. Respond to the Cry of the Prophets
Jesus responds to John's question in a very human and real way. He says to the disciples to tell John that the blind regain sight, lepers walk, and the Good News is for people who really need healing, love, and hope.

This week's gospel reading expresses our human need for God. God comes into the world to heal us. We are still in need of this healing. To find God means we also are in relationship with people who continue to need this healing within our communities. We are called to become vulnerable to people in need, those who cannot help themselves.

Consider how are you opening your heart to the needs of people in your community, family, or world. Can you see beyond God's love for you to the dire needs of people living in poverty, the mentally ill, the sick, and the outcast? How is God leading you toward acknowledging the real needs of God's beloved? Take stock of your actions, attitudes, and awareness of your relationship with people living in great need. How is God investing in you a rich source of compassion and integrity?

1. Jesus, I see you work in my life yet I am still blind toward

2. I know I should feel more compassion toward people who have less, yet I

3. Action: I will help today with

Step 5. Prayer: Writing Your Way to New Birth
Take a minute or two to look back at what you have written. Then compose a short prayer offering whatever is in your heart to God. Write it in the space below or in the quiet of your heart and mind.

TUESDAY

Step 1. Welcome the Stranger Called Silence
Settle into your retreat space and sit in silence for a minute or two.

Step 2. Discover Your Story Within the Word
As you make the sign of the cross, pray:

O God, unshelter my heart that I may hear and know your holy Word.

Read the Sunday gospel passage in silence or aloud. Then spend another minute or two in silent reflection on the reading.

What good news do you see and hear that you can tell others?

Step 3. Connect to the Waiting World: Go and Tell What You Hear and See

Reflect on your action from yesterday.

How well have you met that goal?

Step 4. Respond to the Cry of the Prophets

Jesus tells his disciples and the crowd about discovering the action of God among those who suffer. The images of blindness, being crippled, being cleansed from leprosy, and being poor are also ways for us to discover faith and wholeness.

When the trappings of illusion or sin blind us, God opens our eyes to see the miracles of life. When we are crippled by our own selfishness or despair, God allows us to walk in the light of Christ. These images play an important role in opening our hearts to the faith we seek during these Advent weeks. In these images we discover our own earthly poverty.

Try to capture for yourself how the experience of blindness has opened up your life to a greater reality. Try to name an experience of blindness, such as holding a grudge against a spouse, living a lie with a friend, or realizing a prejudice you hold. How does God use these experiences to invite you into a greater depth of compassion and awareness? Are you willing to look beyond the grudge, the lie, or the prejudice to "see" people in a new way?

1. Jesus, I discover my reluctance to "see" people as they truly are because

2. God, help me in my blindness to others so that

3. Action: I will act on my reluctance toward

Step 5. Prayer: Writing Your Way to New Birth
Take a minute or two to look back at what you have written. Then compose a short prayer offering whatever is in your heart to God. Write it in the space below or in the quiet of your heart and mind.

WEDNESDAY

Step 1. Welcome the Stranger Called Silence
Settle into your retreat space and sit in silence for a minute or two.

Step 2. Discover Your Story Within the Word
As you make the sign of the cross, pray:

O God, unshelter my heart that I may hear and know your holy Word.

Read the Sunday gospel passage in silence or aloud. Then spend another minute or two in silent reflection on the reading.

What good news do you see and hear that you can tell others?

Step 3. Connect to the Waiting World: Go and Tell What You Hear and See

Reflect on your action from yesterday.

How well have you met that goal?

Step 4. Respond to the Cry of the Prophets

The heart of Advent waiting lives among people who need God in basic human ways. The longing we all have for God to heal us is lived within community. Jesus says to the crowd that John's prophecy comes in simple ways. The finely robed and the palace dweller may not hear the prophetic words and act upon them.

The revelation of God's love comes in the simple hearts of God's people. Our apathy, ignorance, or neglect keeps us from realizing the birth of love in the world.

Advent claims the poor as the birthplace for real change and the discovery of the miracles of life. In Advent, we realize that God is invested in our own poverty, and in all the ways in which we need love, compassion, and integrity.

In today's reflection, I encourage you to contemplate your own personal poverty in your real-life story: the dark moments of failure, the resistance toward God, the hardships you endure in relationships, and your inability to change your ways. We need God's grace to sustain us. We cannot change these things on our own. Even our prayer comes from God's desire to be with us.

In what ways do you see in your own crippled heart, the longing for freedom and life?

1.   I see my own personal poverty as a way toward

2. I hope for

3. Action: Today, I will take one step toward

Step 5. Prayer: Writing Your Way to New Birth
Take a minute or two to look back at what you have written. Then compose a short prayer offering whatever is in your heart to God. Write it in the space below or in the quiet of your heart and mind.

■ THURSDAY

Step 1. Welcome the Stranger Called Silence
Settle into your retreat space and sit in silence for a minute or two.

Step 2. Discover Your Story Within the Word
As you make the sign of the cross, pray:

O God, unshelter my heart that I may hear and know your holy Word.

Read the Sunday gospel passage in silence or aloud. Then spend another minute or two in silent reflection on the reading.

What good news do you see and hear that you can tell others?

Step 3. Connect to the Waiting World: Go and Tell What You Hear and See

Reflect on your action from yesterday.

How well have you met that goal?

Step 4. Respond to the Cry of the Prophets

John's life was itself a sign pointing to the kingdom of God. He was a prophet bearing the message of God in his every word and deed. Even his clothing and diet were a witness to the reality of God's kingdom. John came to earth bearing the message of God, preparing us all for the life of heaven.

In Advent, we also acknowledge our own prophetic lives bearing witness to God's love and mercy. Through the gift of our own baptism, we follow Christ in every aspect of our lives: our thoughts, words, and actions.

Reflect today on your own role as a prophet. How are you a witness of God's love to your children, your spouse, or neighbor? How do you see your responsibility as one who receives God's love and who is called to live that love in the world? In this Advent we also wait for every believer to acknowledge the gift of faith. We are called to live in these dark days of Advent, the light and life of Christ Jesus. How do you see your heart being opened by Christ's light?

1. I see this gift of my faith leading me to

2. Jesus, help me speak out for people who

3. Action: Today I will accept responsibility for

Step 5. Prayer: Writing Your Way to New Birth

Take a minute or two to look back at what you have written. Then compose a short prayer offering whatever is in your heart to God. Write it in the space below or in the quiet of your heart and mind.

FRIDAY

Step 1. Welcome the Stranger Called Silence
Settle into your retreat space and sit in silence for a minute or two.

Step 2. Discover Your Story Within the Word
As you make the sign of the cross, pray:

O God, unshelter my heart that I may hear and know your holy Word.

Read the Sunday gospel passage in silence or aloud. Then spend another minute or two in silent reflection on the reading.

What good news do you see and hear that you can tell others?

Step 3. Connect to the Waiting World: Go and Tell What You Hear and See
Reflect on your action from yesterday.

How well have you met that goal?

Step 4. Respond to the Cry of the Prophets

One of the major themes for Advent is gratitude for our lives and the life of the world. As we ponder the message of waiting for the Messiah, we know of course that the Messiah has already come into the world. The presence of Christ is among us still in the gift of the Holy Spirit.

The Holy Spirit offers us grace to open our hearts to the needs of the world. We become instruments of God's love relying on the gift of the Spirit. Faith alone removes whatever obstacles in our heart keep us from being instruments of love and healing within all our relationships. We ask God for continued grace to live with a new awareness of people's needs.

In your prayer today, turn humbly toward God. Allow God to love you into service among God's people. Be grateful—even in our world faced with hardship, poverty, and the horror of war. God depends on each of us to be an instrument of justice and peace, which begins with a heart that knows the healing love of Christ Jesus. Ask the Holy Spirit for courage in your belief.

1. The message I need to tell others about Advent is

2. I received from God

3. Action: Today I will contact _____, because

Step 5. Prayer: Writing Your Way to New Birth

Take a minute or two to look back at what you have written. Then compose a short prayer offering whatever is in your heart to God. Write it in the space below or in the quiet of your heart and mind.

SATURDAY

Step 1. Welcome the Stranger Called Silence
Settle into your retreat space and sit in silence for a minute or two.

Step 2. Discover Your Story Within the Word
As you make the sign of the cross, pray:

O God, unshelter my heart that I may hear and know your holy Word.

Read the Sunday gospel passage in silence or aloud. Then spend another minute or two in silent reflection on the reading.

What good news do you see and hear that you can tell others?

Step 3. Connect to the Waiting World: Go and Tell What You Hear and See
Reflect on your action from yesterday.

How well have you met that goal?

Step 4. Respond to the Cry of the Prophets

As believers we rejoice in God's presence even in the midst of all that is unresolved. We believe Christ is already among us, and we rejoice in God's love. However, we wait for healing of the sick, encouragement for the downcast, and hope for the marginalized.

In Advent, we straddle between life on earth and the life to come. This is the mystery of our faith: that Christ is among us and yet will not be fully revealed until the end of time. Here, we rejoice in God's love that guides us through the path of life to our place in eternity.

Today, pray with all your heart and rejoice in God's love for you. As your heart expands to full awareness of the world's needs and suffering, rejoice in the love and in all that remains unresolved on Earth. We wait in joyful hope for the coming of Christ Jesus.

1. Jesus, allow my life to speak of your love so

2. I rejoice today in

3. Action: Today, I will stop and appreciate the world in which I live by

Step 5. Prayer: Writing Your Way to New Birth

Take a minute or two to look back at what you have written. Then compose a short prayer offering whatever is in your heart to God. Write it in the space below or in the quiet of your heart and mind.

Prayer for the Third Week of Advent

Jesus,
I feel the frigid air seeping between the steel-framed windows.
The fresh snow under the streetlights reflects more light in the city.
The cold morning stirs my hot anger about how people fought off the frigid night.

Only you help me not to find my identity amid people's misfortunes.
You are the one I seek because I no longer trust my own thoughts and reactions.
Your life teaches me to live amid the shackles of people's suffering.

My silence today invites me deeper into my own deafness.
My limping prayer staggers along the path of my fear.
Blind longing for you unveils my desire to see your saving face.

In these Advent days, I slowly find my heart awake and singing.
Faith creeps out of the cracks of my soul from my uncertainty.
Gratitude lights up the morning inside me and relaxes my silence in my still body.
Amen.

God Is with Us

SUNDAY

Step 1. Welcome the Stranger Called Silence
Settle into your retreat space and sit in silence for a minute or two.

Step 2. Discover Your Story Within the Word
As you make the sign of the cross, pray:

O God, unshelter my heart that I may hear and know your holy Word.

Read the gospel passage in silence or aloud.

Matthew 1:18–24
Now this is how the birth of Jesus Christ came about. When his mother Mary was betrothed to Joseph, but before they lived together, she was found with child through the Holy Spirit.
Joseph her husband, since he was a righteous man, yet unwilling to expose her to shame, decided to divorce her quietly.
Such was his intention when, behold, the angel of the Lord appeared to him in a dream and said,

"Joseph, son of David, do not be afraid to take Mary your wife into your home. For it is through the Holy Spirit that this child has been conceived in her. She will bear a son and you are to name him Jesus, because he will save his people from their sins." All this took place to fulfill what the Lord had said through the prophet: "Behold, the virgin shall be with child and bear a son, and they shall name him Emmanuel," which means "God is with us." When Joseph awoke, he did as the angel of the Lord had commanded him and took his wife into his home.

Spend another minute or two in silent reflection on the reading.

Step 3. Connect to the Waiting World: God Is with Us

I walk along our neighborhood sidewalks that are littered with broken dreams. Drug dealers chase down cars in the early morning. Prostitutes stand silently on the corner of the block. The rain and cold do not deter people from lining up at our chapel door before dawn. The long-term dreams of people experiencing poverty seldom come true. Their ideas of how life should have turned out scatter like crumbs on our sidewalk.

I carry these moments to the dying and rising of Christ. This is the only place that makes sense for me to continue dreaming. This is the place in which new birth for people can happen. I stand in great hope on our streets because even the original plan of Joseph and Mary did not work according to their hopes.

I relish the fact that Joseph acted upon his new dream. He must have thought that his human dreams with Mary had been shattered. His plan for marriage and family was not going to be realized, at least not in the way he thought. Then in the center of his torment, an angel brought news that he was to continue with his plans. The angel legitimized his original dream and assured him that he need not fear.

The pregnancy of Mary and the dreams of Joseph offer us the potential for new life and our own share of love. Mary's pregnancy is also the gift that allowed her an inner trust that life would continue even with the threat of cultural laws that forbade sex before marriage. Joseph's dream is a gift from God restoring his inner trust that his life was back on track.

I cling to their human relationship and their relationship with God as I struggle in our day to find a room in the inn for our folks who line up waiting for hot food, clean socks, and a laundry voucher to wash their few items of clothing. I believe the sustaining answer revolves around our ability to act fearlessly. In Advent we are called to hear and see God's love being born within the world and us. For all of us to birth hope into a waiting world, we must let go of fear. We cannot be afraid to serve people who most need to have fulfilled the simple dreams of survival, food, shelter, healing, and life-sustaining relationships.

Every year by this point in Advent, I realize that God is trying desperately to restore my own inner life, my ability to trust the power of grace that is at the center of my being. This new life takes time and patience. I cannot give to others what I have not discovered myself. To act in service among people on the margins, I must come to the center of love myself. I must allow God to continue to energize my service by forgiving my stubbornness, loving my brokenness, and healing my despair.

The real beauty and treasure of Advent for every Christian community are that faith is about real people and honest relationships. The incarnation of love comes through the hope and dreams of God for all humanity. This love calls each of us to learn that the barriers we erect between one another must be replaced with a new desire to serve, listen, and love people. The presence of Christ also challenges every person and community to break down the notion that people are different because some people possess more than others: money, power, prestige, education, or even notoriety.

Advent leads us to the fact that Christ promised to remain with us forever. Advent is the firm conviction that love has not left our neighborhoods and that hope comes through our own turning to God. If we are to remain in God's love and to celebrate the mystery of Christ in our midst, then we must be able to treat others with mutual respect and dignity. Christ who was born on the margins of the city comes to the center of life when we reach out to people who are lost and longing for a room in the inn of our lives.

Emmanuel, or God with us, remains not just a pious thought but also the rich and radical notion that all life has meaning and that love is available for all people. If we believe that God is still among us, then we shall be taken to the places where life seems empty, ignored, and forgotten. Advent wakes up every Christian community to discover that we are all waiting for the same things: to be loved, known, and cared for in the promises of Christ Jesus, yesterday, today, and tomorrow. Come, Lord, Jesus!

Step 4. Respond to the Cry of the Prophets

The emphasis of the gospel reading shifts in this fourth week of Advent. The ancient cries of the prophets are quieted by the pregnancy of Mary. We wait now among the dreams of Joseph and the words of angels. We wait for our own fears to be cast aside as we wait for Emmanuel, God with us.

The angel arrives in Joseph's dream just in time to calm him about his future. Every time an angel appears in the gospels, the angel reveals a new presence of Christ. Here, of course, we wait for the birth of the long-awaited one.

In these last days of Advent, I invite you into prayer to focus on your fears. How is God calling you into a deeper awareness of love, and what fear do you carry with you? As you prepare to be with loved ones this week, what fear keeps rising in your heart? As you scurry around with last-minute preparations for Christmas, what fears keep you downcast? Prepare for the celebration of Christmas this week by admitting your fears and praying through the mystery of all that is unresolved in your heart.

1.   Jesus, as Christmas draws near, the fears that arise in me seem

2. God, receive my life and the questions of my heart and

3. Action: Today I will take one step to share my fear of

Step 5. Prayer: Writing Your Way to New Birth

Take a minute or two to look back at what you have written. Then compose a short prayer offering whatever is in your heart to God. Write it in the space below or in the quiet of your heart and mind.

MONDAY

Step 1. Welcome the Stranger Called Silence

Settle into your retreat space and sit in silence for a minute or two.

Step 2. Discover Your Story Within the Word

As you make the sign of the cross, pray:

O God, unshelter my heart that I may hear and know your holy Word.

Read the Sunday gospel passage (pp. 69–70) in silence or aloud. Then spend another minute or two in silent reflection on the reading.

Where do you experience God with us?

Step 3. *Connect to the Waiting World: God Is with Us*

You may wish to revisit the thematic essay on pages 70–72 if it will help you focus your retreat time.

Take a couple of minutes to think about how well you did with your action from yesterday. Journal about it if that is useful.

Step 4. *Respond to the Cry of the Prophets*

Advent invites us into the dreams of the Holy Family and the dreams God has for all creation. We wait for these dreams to be fulfilled in the presence and sight of Christ among us.

Joseph's dream was very directive. He heard immediately from God the choices he had to make for his new family. Our dreams may not be so easy or may not come true as we plan for them to.

My prayer for you today is that you dream for yourself and the world. I encourage you to dream big dreams. Dream that you may finally discover in your unsheltered heart the dwelling place of God. Dream that the world in all its fragile ways may realize the abiding love God has for everyone. Dream about your family's needs, and dream about people in every land and nation begging for the peace that only God can bring.

1. God, allow me to dream for myself that

2. Today, if I could dream one dream for the world it
    would be

3. Action: Today, I will act on one dream I have for my
    family:

Step 5. Prayer: Writing Your Way to New Birth

Take a minute or two to look back at what you have written. Then compose a short prayer offering whatever is in your heart to God. Write it in the space below or in the quiet of your heart and mind.

TUESDAY

Step 1. Welcome the Stranger Called Silence
Settle into your retreat space and sit in silence for a minute or two.

Step 2. Discover Your Story Within the Word
As you make the sign of the cross, pray:

O God, unshelter my heart that I may hear and know your holy Word.

Read the gospel passage in silence or aloud. Then spend another minute or two in silent reflection on the reading.

Where do you experience God with us?

Step 3. Connect to the Waiting World: God Is with Us
Reflect on your action from yesterday.

How well have you met that goal?

Step 4. Respond to the Cry of the Prophets

After Joseph's dream, his priority was his immediate family. In this season of love, our hearts turn to our families. No matter whom we call family—our family of origin or close friends—we become aware of people we love. Our priorities, our travel, and our preparations all point to the people we love and with whom we hope to celebrate in this season.

Advent allows us to see again the beauty of people we love. Our hearts ache to be with people whom we love and who love us. Of course this is not always possible for many people.

Financial concerns, travel plans, recent breakups in relation-ships, and the death of loved ones create a shift in how we plan our holiday observances.

Today, I encourage you to sit in prayer for those you love and for people who cannot be with you during this season. Make prayer your first priority in how you plan your celebra-tions. Take quiet time to pray even in this busiest time of the year. People you love are your first priority, whether or not you will be with them for the actual observance of Christmas.

1. My prayer for the people I love today is

2. My prayer for friends and family who will not be present with me is

3. Action: Today, I will contact one friend whom I will not be with this Christmas:

Step 5. Prayer: Writing Your Way to New Birth

Take a minute or two to look back at what you have written. Then compose a short prayer offering whatever is in your heart to God. Write it in the space below or in the quiet of your heart and mind.

WEDNESDAY

Step 1. Welcome the Stranger Called Silence
Settle into your retreat space and sit in silence for a minute or two.

Step 2. Discover Your Story Within the Word
As you make the sign of the cross, pray:

O God, unshelter my heart that I may hear and know your holy Word.

Read the gospel passage in silence or aloud. Then spend another minute or two in silent reflection on the reading.

Where do you experience God with us?

Step 3. Connect to the Waiting World: God Is with Us
Reflect on your action from yesterday.

How well have you met that goal?

Step 4. Respond to the Cry of the Prophets

This joyous season of Advent—even with the stress of work, planning, and the emotional worries of people gathering again—brings us the realization that all of life is a gift. The presence of Christ reminds us that God cares for us and for all of creation. We give presents at Christmas to remind us that God gives us life itself.

The final days of Advent may bring worry, travel, and unexpected concerns, but the reality of our preparation continues. All life is God's grace-filled offering to us. The good, the bad, th unresolved choices, and the uncertain future all come to us at this time wrapped as our human lives. Here in Advent we must let ourselves enter into the mystery that is the Incarnation, revealing love in all we are and hope to become.

Spend quiet time today with your child, grandchild, neighbor, or friend. Allow this encounter to be your prayer. Take time to relish these relationships and speak this gratitude to your loved one. Now is the time to act out of God's goodness toward you. Now is the time to be grateful for every moment of your life.

1. I now see the face of God in

2. I need to tell _____ about the true gifts that God is giving me so

3. Action: Today I will contact _____

Step 5. Prayer: Writing Your Way to New Birth

Take a minute or two to look back at what you have written. Then compose a short prayer offering whatever is in your heart to God. Write it in the space below or in the quiet of your heart and mind.

THURSDAY

Step 1. Welcome the Stranger Called Silence
Settle into your retreat space and sit in silence for a minute or two.

Step 2. Discover Your Story Within the Word
As you make the sign of the cross, pray:

O God, unshelter my heart that I may hear and know your holy Word.

Read the gospel passage in silence or aloud. Then spend another minute or two in silent reflection on the reading.

Where do you experience God with us?

Step 3. Connect to the Waiting World: God Is with Us
Reflect on your action from yesterday.

How well have you met that goal?

Step 4. Respond to the Cry of the Prophets

The angel in Joseph's dream was preparing the place and circumstances of Jesus' birth. The angel, in fact, was preparing the marriage of God and all humanity. This feast is still going on; the love of God is still manifesting itself among us.

This Advent readies us for a great feast, a celebration of God made flesh. Unfortunately we do not have angels helping us make the actual meals and washing the dishes. We do not have angels to end violence or hatred, neglect or tragedy.

We do have the power of God's grace within us to truly make this season a real feast of kindness, hospitality, and peace for many people.

Today, tend to the preparations if you are hosting a meal for family or friends. Make the preparations your prayer. Be conscious of who will be in your home. Think about what has happened to your family or friends this past year. Make all these stories your prayer. Allow the people, the circumstances, the happiness, or unhappiness to sink into your heart. Allow your heart to be stripped of anger, unkindness, and judgment. This is the incarnation of love.

1. Today, I will prepare a hospitable place for

2. I still need to let go of my attitude of

3. Action: Today, I will prepare my heart for people I love by

Step 5. Prayer: Writing Your Way to New Birth

Take a minute or two to look back at what you have written. Then compose a short prayer offering whatever is in your heart to God. Write it in the space below or in the quiet of your heart and mind.

FRIDAY

Step 1. Welcome the Stranger Called Silence
Settle into your retreat space and sit in silence for a minute or two.

Step 2. Discover Your Story Within the Word
As you make the sign of the cross, pray:

O God, unshelter my heart that I may hear and know your holy Word.

Read the gospel passage in silence or aloud. Then spend another minute or two in silent reflection on the reading.

Where do you experience God with us?

Step 3. Connect to the Waiting World: God Is with Us
Reflect on your action from yesterday.

How well have you met that goal?

Step 4. Respond to the Cry of the Prophets

Advent is a journey toward a new awareness of Emmanuel, God with us. God's life here on earth is constantly renewing God's people. We have spent the Advent season naming the obstacles that shield our hearts from love, compassion, and kindness toward others. This process is a journey that takes us a lifetime to consider.

Our unsheltered hearts now are exposed lovingly to the grace of God. We hold the mystery of life in our hearts—the tragic and the gentle, the corrupt and the beautiful, the dark and the loving. As we gather at the Eucharist to celebrate Emmanuel, God with us, we know that love is present. As we feast in prayer with our parish communities and families, we see God's activity, even within life's paradoxes, with new eyes and a new love for our world.

"Behold, the virgin shall be with child and bear a son, and they shall name him Emmanuel," which means "God is with us."

1. Today, on Christmas Eve, gratitude fills my heart because

Step 5. Prayer: Writing Your Way to New Birth
Take a minute or two to look back at what you have written. Then compose a short prayer offering whatever is in your heart to God. Write it in the space below or in the quiet of your heart and mind.

Prayer for the Fourth Week of Advent

Jesus,
I hold the shards of broken dreams in my awkward
silence.
These jagged reminders tell me that countless plans and
ideas shatter.
Many of the shredded dreams of people are not their
fault.

Remove the heavy debris from my disappointed heart.
Restore my inner life with your love as you did for
Mary and Joseph.
Inspire me to live from the grace of your dream for me.

Carry all my misfortunes to your death and
resurrection.
Lift the guilt I carry for not responding to the dreams of
others.
In these silent moments birth in me a more loving
heart.

Do not leave me in my silence to travel alone.
I trust that you are dreaming for others in my pregnant
silence.
Emmanuel, at last, you are my hope for a new
morning.
Amen.

Ronald Patrick Raab, C.S.C., ministers among the vulnerable and marginalized of society and the Church. From his experiences in living the Gospel among the poor, he speaks and writes about prayer and service and knowing the love of God through our common poverty. He hosts *On the Margins*, a weekly radio scripture commentary on KBVM 88.3 FM, Catholic Broadcasting Northwest. He is active as a retreat director, workshop presenter, blogger, and award-winning author. He contributes regularly to several liturgy magazines, including *Ministry & Liturgy* and *Celebrate!* Raab serves as associate pastor at the Downtown Chapel in Portland, Oregon. Visit Raab online at ronaldraab.blogspot.com.

Founded in 1865, Ave Maria Press,
a ministry of the Congregation of
Holy Cross, is a Catholic publishing
company that serves the spiritual and
formative needs of the Church and its
schools, institutions, and ministers;
Christian individuals and families; and
others seeking spiritual nourishment.

———

For a complete listing of titles from

Ave Maria Press

Sorin Books

Forest of Peace

Christian Classics

visit www.avemariapress.com

ave maria press® / Notre Dame, IN 46556
A Ministry of the Indiana Province of Holy Cross